Academic Quicksand

THE PROFESSIONAL EDUCATION SERIES

Walter K. Beggs, *Editor*
Dean Emeritus Teachers College, and
Professor of Educational Administration
University of Nebraska

Royce H. Knapp, *Research Editor*
Regents Professor of Education
Teachers College
University of Nebraska

Academic Quicksand

Some Trends and Issues in Higher Education

Vice President and Dean of the University
Illinois State University

and

STANLEY G. RIVES

Dean of Undergraduate Instruction
Illinois State University

PROFESSIONAL EDUCATORS PUBLICATIONS, INC.
LINCOLN, NEBRASKA

Library of Congress Catalog Card No.: 72-97767

ISBN   0-88224-037-4

Contents

5

Introduction

Few public officials — appointed or elected — have a more diverse constituency than today's college and university administrator, and the demands upon him are often excessive and unrealistic.*

For example, there are students who expect him to interpret their wishes in the most liberal terms possible and believe it only right that he should support them always on the sensitive issues of self-determination.

There are faculty members who expect him to champion unequivocally the complex, and frequency unpopular, causes of academic freedom with such critical groups as governing boards and legislatures.

There are trustees who expect the administrator to have faculty members teach more and research less, and have students adhere to more traditional or historically accepted norms.

There are governors and state legislators who expect him to do more and better things with existing budget resources, while disposing of academically acceptable, but economically questionable, programs.

There are citizens who expect him to bring order out of universal chaos on the campus in volatile areas such as collective bargaining of faculty, student behavior, and marketability of collegiate programs and graduates.

There are other demanding constituents, too.

In the pages which follow the authors have attempted to set out what the various groups generally expect of their academic administrator. The expectations are staggering, but in order for one to succeed — or even survive — he must have a reasonable comprehension of them, regardless of their relevance.

7

As the title indicates, there are very real dangers in the profession of academic administration. Certain ones can be fatal professionally; others can be crippling for both the administrator and the institution. Therefore, the authors have tried to identify likely pools of academic quicksand and the legitimate expectations of the modern college and university administrator.

*Logan Wilson, *Shaping American Higher Education* (Washington, D.C.: American Council on Education, 1972). The authors recommend this work, believing that it gives additional insight into a number of the subjects which they have explored.

CHAPTER 1

What Students Expect

The American college student enters the academy for a variety of complex reasons. He is there because his parents expect him to be, but also because college provides independence from family, because he is vaguely uncertain of what to do with his life or because he has a precise vocational goal which requires a college education, because he isn't ready to start work (or enter military service) and the society doesn't seem to offer much in the way of meaningful employment to the eighteen-year-old high school graduate, because his friends are in college and his parents and teachers have urged him to "make something of himself," because he is terribly idealistic in searching for self-identity and self-fulfillment, because some institution awarded him a scholarship for his athletic prowess or scholastic ability which he feels he really should use, because he isn't ready to get married and settle into the rest of the establishment routine and sees college as an experimental life-style which should be experienced as part of one's youth, because he really expects to learn and know and discover and assert his individuality. Above all, he is there *because he wants to learn.*

Perhaps the best profile of the contemporary American college student is sketched by the Committee on the Student in Higher Education:

1. Students are seeking commitments but are skeptical about the ideologies and orthodoxies that clamor for their loyalty.

2. Because of their suspicion about formal ideology, the new students turn to human relationships as the source of most of the purpose and meaning they seek in their lives.

9

3. The contemporary college student feels strongly the need to belong but is profoundly skeptical about most of the organizations he encounters, particularly an organization that claims to offer him an education.

4. The new student is generous and idealistic in his own fashion but is frequently fearful that any long-term commitment to social service may destroy his idealism and thwart his freedom.

5. The new students, for all their apparent poise and sophistication, are frequently hesitant and uncertain.

6. Because of his doubts about himself, about organizations, and the possibility of faith and commitments, the new college student has a tendency to be suspicious and distrustful of the administration, and to a lesser extent, the faculty of his college.

7. Students come to college with a great deal of excitement and willingness to do the work demanded of them, but their expectations and performance usually decline very rapidly during the first months of the freshman year.

8. Most students apparently expect that the college years will mark the definitive end of their dependence on their parents.[1]

GENERAL STUDENT SATISFACTION, DISSATISFACTION, AND EXPECTATIONS

Despite his reservations about society, including his college and his personal adequacy, today's student is largely satisfied with the adventure of learning in college. In the largest survey of academic opinion ever made (including 70,000 undergraduates and 30,000 graduate students), the Carnegie Commission on Higher Education discovered that in an overall evaluation of their colleges, 66 percent of students are "satisfied" or "very satisfied," 22 percent are "on the fence," and 12 percent are "dissatisfied" or "very dissatisfied."[2] Only 5 percent of current college students feel they would be happier if they had never attended college.

The level of satisfaction varies by size of institution (from 71 percent in the satisfied group in institutions of over 10,000 students down to 60 percent in institutions below 1,000 students), by field of study of the undergraduate student (77 percent are satisfied in the physical sciences, 75 in biological sciences, 69 in education and social welfare fields, 63 in social sciences, and 59 percent in humanities), and by type as well as quality of instruction (64 percent of junior college students are in the satisfied group, 63 percent of students in low-quality four-year institutions are satisfied as against 71 in medium-quality and 67 in high-quality four-year institutions, and 63 percent in low-quality universities as against 71 in medium- and 80 in high-quality universities).

A similar picture emerges for graduate students; 77 percent "strongly agree" or "agree with reservations" that they are basically satisfied with the graduate education they are getting. Eighty percent of graduate students report that they are satisfied with their undergraduate preparation in their subject field, although this varies by field (87 percent for health, 83 for both engineering and education/social welfare, 80 for law, 77 for physical sciences, 76 for social sciences, 72 for biological sciences, and 71 for humanities).

These Carnegie Commission findings of the level of student satisfaction in the United States are consistent with a contemporary poll of British students which indicates that 80 percent are generally satisfied with life as a student. They are also consistent with a recent Gallup Poll in which the following proportions of college students gave favorable (good or excellent) ratings to these American institutions: universities, 68 percent; family, 58; business and Congress and the courts, all 56; police, 46; high schools, 37; organized religion, 33; and political parties, 18 percent.

As might be expected, students identify a number of areas in which their colleges and universities need improvement. Undergraduate students indicate they have not "had enough" outlets for creative activities (55 percent), personal contacts with faculty (49), advice and guidance from faculty and staff (47), and freedom in course selection (40 percent). Among the specific items of dissatisfaction listed by undergraduates are variety of courses available (44 percent dissatisfied), quality of classroom instruction (33), faculty-student relations (30), and the intellectual environment (30 percent). Graduate students express desires for more variety in course offerings (51 percent), higher quality of classroom instruction (46), more relevance of course offerings to their future occupation (38), greater availability of faculty to graduate students (34), better knowledge of where graduate students stand academically (33), less wasteful repetition between undergraduate and graduate work (32), and less research orientation in their fields (27 percent).

Undergraduate students and faculty respond in the following ways to specific suggestions for reform in higher education. The percentages express agreement with the statement that undergraduate education in America would be improved if—

	STUDENT AGREEMENT	FACULTY AGREEMENT
1. All courses were elective.	51%	19%
2. Grades were abolished.	59	33
3. Coursework were more relevant to contemporary life and problems.	91	75
4. More attention were paid to the emotional growth of students.	83	71
5. Students were required to spend a year in community service in the United States or abroad.	48	56
6. There were less emphasis on specialized training and more on broad liberal education.	37	56
7. Teaching effectiveness, not publications, were the primary criterion for promoting of faculty.	95	78

The college administrator should note well the fact that there is significant faculty and student agreement that teaching should be the primary criterion in faculty promotion, that course work should be more relevant to contemporary life and problems, and that more attention should be paid in higher education to the emotional growth of students.

What do students expect of college administrators? Students would never phrase the question this way. Rather their question would simply be, what do students expect of their college or university? The reason for the rephrasing is that most college students (student government leaders are a notable exception) are only vaguely aware of administrators. Student contact is largely with faculty and other students, not the bureaucratic structure of administration. When asked to identify the chairman of the department in which he majored, a typical junior student in a large Midwestern university replied, "I haven't met him although I think I remember him talking to us during freshman orientation." Asked also about his college dean, the student replied, "Where is his office?" The one administrative officer most students can consistently identify on a campus is the president, although they have a rather vague concept about what it is that he does. The bulk of student contact is with faculty members.

In fact, a large percentage of the student contact with administrators which does occur happens when the student runs afoul of the system — when his grade-point average endangers his status as a student, when his academic adviser can't handle a needed exception to curriculum requirements, when he has a complaint about being required to live in a dormitory. Otherwise, students are likely to view administration as a system, not as individuals. And if the system really frustrates them enough, they are likely as not to go to the president's office for resolution. It is possible, however, to identify major student concerns and expectations of the institution, and hence its administration. Interviews with students reveal that among the major expectations in rough priority are a good teaching faculty, a range of high-quality academic programs, some opportunity to have a voice in the college decisions which affect their lives, and a responsive administrative bureaucratic structure.[3]

STUDENTS AND THE TEACHING FACULTY

Students have very high expectations of faculty, which they are quite willing to express. Listening to what contemporary students say they want from their instructors can be useful for faculty, but also for administrators responsible for recruiting new faculty and rewarding faculty members who meet student expectations. While this consumer orientation may not always influence the content of instruction, it may well have a significant impact upon faculty attitudes and approaches to teaching. Among the student expectations of faculty:[4]

"I would hope the professors could understand that the student is actually a human being in disguise. Students are not computers into which information is poured and the desired product regurgitated."

"I am very insecure about many things, even myself and my actions. Sometimes these things make me emotionally unstable and I feel very alone and lonely. If my professors understood this and knew that I tried my hardest, I would feel much better about college life." "I'm not just sure what I want out of life, or what life wants out of me," but "I'm terribly concerned about my future in this tight job market." "I'm scared and confused. I'm out on my own really for the first time so I'm not sure how much time I should spend studying and how much time having fun. I would like them (professors) to be patient until I get things straight for myself."

"College professors have a reputation of being hard-guys, never really involved with their students. I think I need to feel involved." "Everyone should be involved. Every student should feel that his courses are made for him and that the class cannot go on without his physical and mental participation." "I expect courses and professors to be more personal, involving me as an individual."

"To teach you must be understanding. Have control but don't be afraid to reach out and be yourself. This way we can learn about human relationships — and what else really matters?"

"I would like the professors to understand my problems as I see them. Just being black creates problems in itself in this society." "I am an individual and the way I dress, act, or feel should in no way disturb the way the professor teaches me." "Please remember I am a human being. Do not fold, spindle, or mutilate."

"I'll be looking for the professor who cares whether students flunk or pass, are happy or sad." "If a teacher notices me and is pleased with my desire to learn, I would be extremely upset if I felt I let that teacher down." "I want my professor to have time for me as a friend as well as a student. This means much more than simply knowing and teaching his materials; books can do that."

"If professors talk like their subject is important and act like they enjoy their work, I will enjoy their classes." "What excites me in learning most is when a teacher himself is super-excited by teaching his subject and (very important) knows so much about it that he can answer any question." "When I know a teacher likes teaching his class, I figure there's got to be something I can get out of it." "I expect professors to know exactly what they are talking about."

"The worst professor is the one who is more interested in finishing his personal work than teaching students." "He shouldn't make me feel he would rather be somewhere else." "It is important that the teacher keep his identity and not act like a freshman in college himself." "Everyone needs sleep. If the teaching is boring, I'll get mine in class."

"I like a teacher who cares. He gives you the results of your tests promptly and helps you learn by your mistakes." The best professor is "demanding yet willing to accept the student as he is" and "willing to discuss problems other than academic, leaving his office door open to any questions or problems I may have."

"If a professor would guide me into learning instead of taking my hand and pulling me through, it would let me want to learn. In other words, let me discover for myself."

Today's college student wants a college professor who knows his discipline and can do a good job of communicating knowledge and answering student questions, who is deeply interested or even excited about his subject, who demonstrates interest in students as individuals and is willing to talk with them about social and emotional as well as academic problems, who understands the insecurities of students and cares about human interaction, who is vitally interested in teaching, who demonstrates intellectual rigor tempered with human understanding and a willingness to lead students down paths of self-discovery.

The parents of students also echo this concern. "Providing good instruction," says one father, "is the prime contribution of any center of learning." Other parents state: "We expect the university to hire as many fine teachers as possible, so our youngsters will have the opportunity to receive the best education"; "Give him a well-rounded education, not just academic"; "Give our kids professors who like to teach, and who are not primarily interested in research or publishing just for their own sake"; "Recognize that a lot of young people are not as sure of themselves as they indicate, and show compassion for them"; "Teach him to learn, to live together with other people, and to be a man." There is even parental idealism many view as the exclusive province of youth. "Convince our sons and daughters that there is still hope for mankind," says one parent, for while "we have many problems in the world, we also have many tools to solve the problems."

Implicit in the demands of students (and even their parents) of the faculty is an administrative expectation. It is the college administrator who is expected to assure that the college or university has the kind of faculty who will be responsive to these student demands. That means identifying and hiring competent faculty; it also means creating a reward system which encourages good teaching. The extent of student concern with administrative action to encourage teaching excellence has recently been demonstrated by student demand for student evaluation of teaching, student participation in faculty hiring and tenure and promotion decisions, including student participation on the faculty committees which have traditionally made these decisions. And students expect support from administrators in their campaign for required student course and teaching evaluations and membership on faculty personnel committees. Many faculty, of course, view the evaluation of teaching effectiveness and faculty hiring-promotion-tenure decisions as faculty prerogatives and these faculty members are as unfriendly to administrators as to students who would intrude. Still, a trend is clearly established toward greater student participation in the definition of teaching competence.

STUDENTS AND ACADEMIC PROGRAMS

While most students have demonstrated a clear interest in being in college primarily to learn, they also expect that they will have a high degree of freedom and flexibility in what they study (the curriculum). The following statements are typical of what students say they expect of college and academic programs:

"I worked hard for several years to earn money for my college education. I want to learn as much as possible." "I'm interested in learning, not wasting my time" and "I'm not here to 'goof off.'" "I care about learning and I'm not here just to please my parents." "I'm willing and eager to learn and I'm not going to college just for something to do."

"I'm here to learn and to have fun. I think it's possible to do both in a classroom." "I do want to learn but also have a good time at it. I guess I want this to be the best four years of my life." "After being out of college for three years, I chose to return and am not interested in goofing around but in getting a good education."

"I don't want to teach.
I don't want a degree.
I don't want a good job.
I just want to paint.
Show me."

"I am a person who has feelings about things such as sex, interracial dating, people getting together, pollution, war, or whatever. I should not be put down for my feelings, morals, or ideas. I am not a child anymore and I have been out into the world and I can see I will have to get involved."

"It's more fun to learn when the individual is encouraged to take the initiative and find things out for himself."

"Give me freedom. Freedom to find what about a certain course interests me and then freedom to pursue that. Freedom to work independently, develop my own individualized course within the standard courses. Freedom to err, freedom to enjoy what I do, and most important, freedom to be honest."

And, worth repeating: "If a professor would guide me into learning instead of taking my hand and pulling me through, it would make me want to learn. In other words, let me discover for myself." The desire to learn coupled with the desire for curricular self-determination, while it characterizes the direction of higher education, is by no means universal. Many a student still wants a prescribed curriculum. Many a male student is still in college to avoid the draft. Many a female student is still in college primarily to find a desirable mate. And the whole concept of curricular flexibility is still much more attractive to students (and faculty) in the humanities and social sciences rather than the physical and natural sciences and highly sequential fields like mathematics. Still, the trend toward curricular flexibility and individualization demanded by students is well established in higher education. One writer, Lewis Mayhew, thus views the general education experience of the typical college student in the next decade:

> But although all students will work generally in the area of the humanities, social sciences, natural sciences and communicative arts, they will not necessarily do so in formal courses organized in orthodox groupings of one teacher and 30 or 40 students. Much of the formal curricula will be offered through independent study which will begin during the freshman year. Students will select a topic which is of interest to them, gain approval of a teacher and then spend considerable time developing it. The project may be a library project but it could as well be a mapping expedition to the Cascades, a teaching experience in a deprived part of the country, the creation of a poem or musical composition, or an ecologically oriented float trip down the Mississippi River. And the reporting—for reporting and synthesis are important parts of education—may be a written paper, a series of photographs, tape recordings or unique artistic statements. As a general rule, the concept of independent study will be so well entrenched by 1980 that every student will spend as much as a third of his undergraduate years working on his own.[5]

Some faculty and even administrators insist that the student desire for curricular freedom and flexibility and relevance (for example, the Carnegie Commission's findings that 91 percent of students want course work more relevant to contemporary life and problems, 59 percent want grades abolished, and 51 percent want all courses to be elective) weakens the fabric of higher education. The faculty, they argue, is responsible for standards of academic excellence and, therefore, a high degree of prescription of what the student should study and when he should study it. Students and more liberal faculty respond that a high degree of student interest may be a precondition to significant learning, that there is no more guarantee of academic rigor in the traditional required course, lecture-discussion syndrome than there is lack of academic standards in independent study or individually tailored curricula. Students, say students, came to college to learn and get a good education and they neither respect nor desire an easy course or professor devoid of rigor and academic excellence. Quality education is what students say they want, and that progressively more means to them a high degree of personal involvement in the educational process—less of the "tell-me-what-you-know-while-I-sit-and-listen-and-take-notes" and more of the "let-me-decide-what-I-should-study-for-I-will-learn-more-if-I-do." The student argument is not that they need faculty less, but that faculty should be more resource persons available as needed for advice and consultation.

If students want increased educational options, they expect administrators to help secure them—sometimes against hostile faculty opinion. The movement tends to be slow and evolutionary with gradual introduction of new options such as the expansion of proficiency examinations, the pass/fail grading system, increased independent study and work-study student internships, an individualized general education program, the introduction of competency-based experiences in lieu of more formal course work, the introduction of a few student-initiated, problem-centered interdisciplinary courses, even the acceptance of a program which allows a student and his faculty adviser to structure an individualized major for the student through some other combination of courses and experiences than is required in existing majors. Each deviation from establishment education is usually accompanied by some combination of broad student and administrative support against a reluctant faculty. While some faculty join the effort, they, alc with administrators, are often viewed by the majority of facu' undermining academic standards and quality to court student favor. Students and administrators have not always been instrumental in involving faculty in the structuring of increased flexibility and the new options. Where this has occurred, the reform has come easier with more real commitment on the part of the faculty to make it work.

STUDENTS AND GOVERNANCE

As students have become more involved in academic concerns, they have become more interested in meaningful involvement in institutional governance, including voting student membership on committees of their departments, college and university committees and senates, and even governing boards. As long as the center of concern of student leadership was with matters like dormitory hours and college regulation of student social activities, a student government organization proved adequate on most campuses. But with the gradual collapse of parietal rules and the demise of the whole *in loco parentis* structure, student governments found themselves with no more battles in this area to win against faculty and administration. When, on one campus, student government prepared to do battle in defense of its third straight request in as many years (the previous two wars were won) for an increase in women's hours in residence halls and the administration responded by doing away with all hours in all residence halls, student government felt vaguely betrayed.

Student leadership, which must be as responsive to its constituency as any other leadership in a democratic society, turned its attention to the newly emerging student interest in academic affairs. First responses were in the context of the existing system. Student governments deliberated and passed resolutions urging academic reform, resolutions aimed at turning the practices of the academy more in the direction of student interest and student values. Interested in more than passing resolutions, student leaders attempting to implement the desires of fellow students soon discovered that while (1) administrative fiat might be all that is re-
· ired to effect a change in hours of residence halls, because the
'ty aren't much involved or concerned, (2) much more than

administrative agreement is required to effect changes in curriculum and grading systems and other academic matters, for these are areas of vital faculty concern and areas which ultimately the faculty, not the administration, effectively control.

While students had been busy organizing students, partly to organize the collective power of students to win the *in loco parentis* battle against administration, faculty had also been busy with establishing their own collective power. Through the pressure of powerful national organizations like the American Association of University Professors, faculty won the right to establish faculty councils or senates on nearly every campus. If determination of disciplinary curricula had long been the prerogative of the faculty, the new faculty councils and senates reconfirmed it by insisting that they be intimately involved in the establishment of all educational policy of the college or university. Shared governance, to faculty, meant that faculty would give the advice on academic matters which administrators would generally be expected to accept and implement.

Student recognition of faculty power in the area of educational policy led directly to the student demand for participation in academic governance. Shared governance, to students, would mean student as well as faculty membership on the college council or university senate. Earl McGrath's *Should Students Share the Power?* summarizes the arguments developed for giving students a formal role in academic government: (1) since education is essential to individual and societal well-being, the academy should reflect the social philosophy and political practices of the larger society where people involved help make decisions, (2) expanded social consciousness — a more serious and informed interest in societal problems — of contemporary students qualifies them for participation in the reform of higher education; (3) the declared objective of colleges and universities to prepare students for responsible participation in a democratic society requires that the academy open its own deliberative bodies to students as a means of preparing them for citizenship; (4) students are as well or better qualified than faculty to correct deficiencies in current curricular offerings by helping bring instruction closer to student interests and needs and the conditions of modern life; (5) decision-making with respect to academic policies as well as personal conduct is an essential aspect of education; and (6) students are uniquely qualified to render certain judgments about the teaching-learning process, particularly the quality of faculty classroom teaching—an area in which other faculty members, administrators, and trustees are not as well qualifed, but which does qualify students to have a voice in selecting staff members and evaluating their professional performance.[6]

The objections of some faculty and administrators to student participation in academic governance, which students have had to overcome where student-faculty governance has been instituted, are (1) students have effected academic change without formal participation in faculty governance and thus either do not need such participation or would be inordinately powerful if allowed formal participation; (2) students, being immature, do not possess the life experience and judgment required in academic deliberations; (3) students are transitory members of the academic community and therefore lack the perspective and commitment required for establishment of long-range academic policies; (4) students lack the specialized knowledge and skill possessed by professional scholars which qualify them to protect and preserve valuable academic traditions; and (5) the responsibilities of studentship do not allow the serious student the time for responsible participation in academic governance.[7]

Administrators have generally supported the movement toward student participation in academic affairs, feeling that students will support academic reform. Some administrators have doubtless supported the movement as a result of direct student pressure to do so and in the hope of balancing faculty control of crucial academic matters. The creation of faculty-student or faculty-student-administration senates is too new a development in higher education to attempt a serious assessment of its impact, although such studies are much needed.

STUDENTS AND ADMINISTRATIVE RESPONSE

The final broad area of student expectation is institutional responsiveness to very specific student needs. As a student works his way through the educational bureaucracy in search of an education, his primary concerns are the quality of faculty teaching and academic programs. Among his other concerns, for which administrators rather than faculty are primarily responsible, are:

1. *Financial assistance.* Many students have always required financial aid (scholarships, student loans, student employment) to complete a college education. As the costs of higher education increase, even more students require financial assistance. Students expect an administrator or administrative office to be available to help them secure the loans and scholarships and employment needed.

2. *Registration process.* What students say they want when it comes to registering for courses is a convenient system. Like most people, they are loath to stand in long lines (the usual college system until recently) to find out that what they want by way of classes of particular professors isn't available. The administrative response has been to computerize the registration process (registration of students for courses is still a much more difficult task than making an airline reservation, although the latter is a much more complex operation of essentially the same type) and do away with the traditional registration line. More sophisticated, many administrators are seeking to make the whole system more responsive to students by attempting to realign course offerings during the preregistration process, that is to offer new sections of courses where there is heavy student demand and canceling other sections in areas of low demand. As higher education becomes more consumer oriented, this approach to registration—offering those courses students want and need as against those courses faculty desire to teach—will become more widespread.

3. *Academic advising.* Traditionally, all or nearly all faculty have been expected to perform the academic advising function. Students, particularly freshmen, have not been satisfied with the quality of this advising. Too often it has meant that the student is expected to come into the faculty member's office with a listing of courses he plans to take that semester, the faculty member does a cursory check of the catalog to see that prerequisites and requirements are being met, and there is little or no real vocational or academic counseling and advising. The Carnegie study, for

example, found that 47 percent of undergraduate students are dissatisfied with "advice and guidance from faculty and staff." As curricula become more flexible and individualized, the level of this student dissatisfaction will increase. Faculty, often preoccupied with their teaching and research activities, generally assign academic advising a low priority. The administrative response, particularly in large institutions, has often been to create a centralized advising service for freshmen or lower division students. And career counseling has tended to receive more emphasis on the campus recently because of the tight job market for college graduates.

4. *Housing.* Except for commuter colleges, students need an inexpensive place to live. Many a residential college responded in the fifties and sixties, when local communities could not absorb the ever-increasing numbers of students in off-campus housing, by building their own dormitories, which they always preferred to label "residence halls." To fill these dorms and pay the bonds which provided the dollars to build them, they simply required students (nearly always freshmen or until age twenty-one) to live in them. Dormitories became the real home of *in loco parentis* and a natural target for student revolt. Students moved out into the community — particularly into apartments — wherever they could where they could pursue a more independent life-style. The administrative response, partly or largely out of economic necessity, has been to attempt to make residence halls more attractive places to live for students. This has meant the abolition of hours and prohibitions against room visits by students of the opposite sex, even coeducational residence halls, and the introduction of educational programs into dormitories with experimental "living-learning" approaches to education.

5. *Specialized programs.* The expansion of educational opportunity with increased access to higher education has resulted in a broader social and economic spectrum of society represented in the typical student body. Less homogeneity among students has created the demand for specialized academic programs, particularly honors programs for the scholastically talented and similar programs for the increasing number of black students and educationally or economically deprived students. Administrators have responded favorably to student demand for such programs while

faculty have often been more interested in how students at both ends of the continuum could be integrated into regular academic programs.

These are only a few of the areas in which students have made new and different demands on colleges and their administrators. Others are in the areas of health services (better medical care for students, availability of birth control information and devices), social programing (better recreational and student union facilities), integration of the campus and the community (new relationships between students and townspeople, student membership on city councils, work-study opportunities in the local community), fewer and more lenient student regulations (allowing residence halls to establish their own minimal rules and regulations, providing a student the opportunity to declare "academic bankruptcy" and begin anew, allowing for student sabbaticals and other easy-in and easy-out access to his college or university), and providing better parking. The focus of these largely non-educational policy issues is likely to be administrative versus student government leadership. That administrators have been largely responsive, either by desire or necessity, in these areas is evidenced by some quite radical innovations introduced in recent years on the campus. Birth control information, for example, is now readily available to the student on nearly every campus in America.

SUMMARY

The American college student for all his anxiety and uncertainty is in college primarily because he wants to learn. He is largely satisfied with his academic experience and inclined to view his college or university as more responsive than other social institutions. He typically is very much aware of faculty and only vaguely aware of administration other than the college president because his daily contacts are with faculty members, not administrators. He becomes aware of administration if he assumes a student leadership position or encounters difficulty in getting through the system.

Students have very high, even unrealistic, expectations of faculty. Above all, they want high-quality instruction characterized by knowledge and enthusiasm of the professor for his discipline. *Teaching* effectiveness is what is important to students and they expect to have a role in evaluating the quality of the teaching of their professors. They are intolerant of being bored in a classroom; they want involvement in the teaching-learning process; they want a professor who demonstrates an interest in them as individuals and who is willing to talk with them about personal as well as academic problems. They even want a voice in determining who will become faculty members and how faculty will be rewarded and promoted.

In academic programs, students want more flexibility, more freedom to determine what they study and how they study it. They desire increased program options, more relevant courses, more independent study and elective opportunities – partly because they feel they will learn more if they study those things in which they are interested. Curricular freedom does not mean lack of academic standards to students; they still respect the intellectual rigor of the tough professor. But they want that professor to be more of a guide to self-discovery and less of a straight lecturer and dispenser of information, which they feel they can get as well when they need it from books.

To effect what they consider needed change in higher education in the area of educational policy, students require a voice in institutional governance. They want voting membership in meaningful numbers on every department, college and university committee, council and senate. They want representation on the board of trustees if that is necessary to achieve their objectives. They have been largely successful in ridding their institutions of parietal rules and regulations – perhaps it did require a student revolt to bury *in loco parentis* in the campus cemetery – but they are beginning to discover that changing the college curriculum is a little like trying to move a cemetery. Administration has largely supported the student demand for educational reform with the faculty fulfilling the role of protector and preserver of academic tradition.

Students also want bureaucratic response to their needs for financial assistance, easy registration processes, better academic advising, good housing, and specialized academic programs. They want to be treated as adult human beings who are not folded, spindled, or mutilated in the process of getting a good education.

NOTES

1. *The Student in Higher Education* (New Haven, Connecticut: Hazen Foundation, 1968), pp. 19-26. The authors provide a discussion of each characteristic.

2. Data in this section all come from the Carnegie Commission on Higher Education's *Reform on Campus: Changing Students, Changing Academic Programs,* June, 1972.

3. This listing is the result of a few intensive discussions with students on the campus of a large public institution in the Midwest, Illinois State University. It should be noted that students consistently referred to what they expect of their institution and did not identify these items as specific responsibilities of administrators. While no attempt was made to secure quantitative data in these interviews, each of the items was mentioned by several of the students interviewed.

4. The quotations of students are all from Gordon Sabine's "What New Students (and Some Parents) Expect of Illinois State University," 1972. The responses are from an open-ended questionnaire administered to 3,800 students in the summer of 1972.

5. Lewis B. Mayhew, "The Future Undergraduate Curriculum," in *Campus 1980: The Shape of the Future in American Higher Education,* ed., Alvin C. Eurich (New York: Dell Publishing Co., 1968), pp. 211-12. Mayhew goes on to describe the impact upon the traditional role of the professor and the student.

6. Earl J. McGrath, *Should Students Share the Power?* (Philadelphia: Temple University Press, 1970), pp. 51-60.

7. This is also a summary of McGrath's excellent discussion of the pros and cons of student participation in his *Should Students Share the Power?* The appendix of this book contains the results of a recent survey of 875 colleges and universities on student participation in governance.

SUPPLEMENTARY REFERENCES

CARNEGIE COMMISSION ON HIGHER EDUCATION. *Reform on Campus: Changing Students, Changing Academic Programs.* New York: McGraw-Hill, 1972.

COMMITTEE ON THE STUDENT IN HIGHER EDUCATION. *The Student in Higher Education.* New Haven: Hazen Foundation, 1968.

MCGRATH, EARL J. *Should Students Share the Power? A Study of Their Role in College and University Governance.* Philadelphia: Temple University Press, 1970.

WOODRING, PAUL. *The Higher Learning in America: A Reassessment.* New York: McGraw-Hill, 1968. See especially "Part Two: Students of the New Era."

CHAPTER 2

What Faculty Expect

Faculty expectations of administrators are conditioned by two significant factors. First, nearly all college administrators are former faculty members, who, given a strong faculty voice in administrative appointments, came to their posts by virtue of sharing academic values with colleagues. A chairman, dean, or presidential candidate disavowing academic freedom and tenure would ordinarily not have the faculty support to warrant appointment. Second, faculty members have a somewhat different set of expectations depending upon the relative closeness or remoteness of the administrators to their own academic unit. A department chairman, for example, is expected to be an articulate advocate of disciplinary interests and needs. While this expectation remains of the academic dean or president, it is moderated by an added responsibility to balance, for example, economic demands of departments against available institutional resources. Indeed, a dean whose faculty appointment is in political science would be deeply suspected in physics or psychology if he persisted in the level of advocacy for the discipline expected of the political science chairman.

Faculty expectations of administrators fall into seven broad categories.[1]

1. *Educational leadership* in the statement of unit goals and in effecting needed change within the academic unit.

2. Fair and just *decision-making*, especially regarding evaluation of faculty performance.

3. Securing the *budget resources* necessary for the unit to operate effectively.

4. Effective *communication*, both internally and externally.

5. *Participatory governance* which allows faculty decisions on educational programing.

6. Protection from *external threats*, particularly in the area of academic freedom.

7. Efficient handling of *routine operations* within the unit, especially personnel and work assignments.

Such expectations are variously expressed in administrative job descriptions. Typical is the following listing of functions of the president contained in one university constitution, which charges the president to be accountable to his board of regents for: conduct of the university in accordance with the governing policies of the board of regents, relevant statutes, and the provisions of the university constitution; effective communication between the board and the university community; preparation of university budgets as necessary for proper planning and reporting; transmission to the board, with his recommendations of proposals inititated within the university, including actions of the academic senate; recruitment and retention of a competent faculty of scholar-teachers and administrators, development of educational programs in accordance with a flexible and evolving academic master plan for the university; development of democratic leadership within the university community; development of rapport between the university and the community in which it is located; and interpretation of the university and its mission to the public.[2]

The superhuman scholar-saint seems often to be sought by administrative search committees, made up largely of faculty, as the following material on "Qualifications" in a letter soliciting candidates for an academic deanship illustrates:

A candidate for Vice President for Academic Affairs at _____ University must have outstanding administrative ability, successful experience as a college or university teacher, an earned doctorate, and evidence of professional competence as manifested by active participation in learned societies and research.

The candidate must show evidence of interest in the problems of academic areas other than his own, commitment to the value of both general and specialized education, vision and decisiveness necessary to assume leadership in the continued development of a total academic program, and the ability to write and speak effectively.

Above all, the candidate should be a person who can work well with and who will be respected by other administrators, faculty, and students. He should be a person who is approachable and who will listen to the views of others. He should be able to modify and adapt his views on the basis of reasoned arguments, but he should also have principles by which he stands. He should have a clear and objective view of his role as the academic leader of the university.

That most administrators satisfactorily fulfill these expectations is demonstrated by a generally high level of faculty satisfaction with both vocation and institution. A national poll, for example, indicates that 91 percent of faculty respond "definitely" or "probably yes" to the question, "If you were to begin your career again, would you still want to be a college professor?" The poll also reveals that in response to the question, "How do you feel about your institution?" again 91 percent indicate that "it is a very good" or "fairly good place for me."[3] Two observations: (1) that one out of ten faculty is dissatisfied with vocational and institutional choice provides a challenge to improved administration and (2) the level of faculty expectation in any of the seven areas will vary depending upon the economic climate and past experience with administrative officers.

EDUCATIONAL LEADERSHIP

No single function of the administration is more important than articulation of institutional goals and problems in need of resolution. This includes the perceptiveness to recognize broad consensus on institutional or unit mission when such agreement exists, and establishing the mechanisms to arrive at such a consensus when it does not already exist. One university president describes this latter process as "setting forth the agenda," while another refers to "making the agenda explicit." Both mean that the chief executive officer of an institution of higher education has a responsibility to articulate the problems facing the institution, delineate the available alternative solutions, involve faculty and students in the discussion and evaluation of those alternatives, advocate acceptance of the most desirable solution which emerges from rigorous analysis, reach the highest level of agreement possible within the community on action necessary to resolve the problem, and then act to implement the community consensus in a fashion which demonstrates a willingness to abide by the consequences of community deliberation once a consensus on decision is reached.

This view of educational leadership admittedly says that those affected by a decision must share in the decision-making process. It is the administrator's responsibility, not to make a unilateral decision, but to direct community attention to critical problems, to provide data and describe possible courses of action, to provide a *process* for rational deliberation, and to exercise the power of the agenda to bring the matter to resolution. Implicit in the process is a knowledge of what issues merit the attention of the group. A department chairman might wisely make a unilateral decision after consultation with individual faculty members on who teaches what course in a given semester or quarter. That chairman, however, would be well-advised to involve his total faculty in extended discussion on changing the nature of departmental major requirements.

While faculty expect to participate in decision-making, ultimately they do not expect to make the decisions themselves. Nor will faculty long tolerate the administrator who refuses to exercise leadership defined as acting to implement needed educational reform. A college administrator should know and be prepared to do something about the facts that of faculty surveyed on what is needed to improve American undergraduate education, 75 percent say it would be improved if "course work were more relevant to contemporary life and problems," 71 percent if "more attention were paid to the emotional growth of students," and 78 percent if "teaching effectiveness, not publications, were the primary criterion for promotion of faculty."[4] These current data dispute some traditional beliefs that "relevant" course work is fadist, that colleges are concerned primarily or even exclusively with intellectual matters, that research and publications, not teaching, are the hallmark of the collegiate scholar-teacher. One specific expectation of the administration, in fact, is a knowledge of the literature of higher education. Faculty, including chairmen, are overwhelmed by the reasonable expectation of "keeping up" with the literature of their disciplines and they generally expect the central administrators to keep them abreast of what is worth knowing in current research and writing on the academy.

FAIR DECISIONS

Faculty reasonably expect that decisions will be made by administrative officers and that these decisions will be fair and just. The absence of decisions is an abdication of leadership which no faculty will long tolerate. A series of decisions unacceptable to the faculty simply requires new leadership. Ultimately, the requirements of "fairness" and "justice" in decision-making include (1) a freedom from personal bias or personal benefit resulting from the decision; (2) a deliberate weighing of alternatives, including an openness to consideration of the relative merits (or disadvantages) of possible courses of action; (3) the existence of a fairly explicit value system upon which decisions are based; and, when necessary, (4) the willingness to explain the rational basis for a decision. Implicit in these requirements is the understanding that values upon which decisions are premised are widely shared in the group. A basic value widely shared in any academic community is a commitment to rationality and open deliberation as a means of improving the human condition. Thus the arbitrary (unilateral) decision is *per se* viewed as the "unjust" or "unfair" administrative decision. A faculty member will generally accept a decision, even if he disagrees, if he feels he has had the opportunity to participate meaningfully in the deliberations prior to the decision and if he can require a rational defense from his administrator.

The evaluation of faculty performance is among the most critical of decisions made by the academic administrator and, therefore, furnishes an excellent illustration of effective administrative decision-making. Negatively, the characteristics of an ineffective chairman in personnel decisions would be easily identifiable. He would use salary recommendations to reward personal friends and punish enemies. He would discourage faculty discussion of such matters as the relative weight assigned to teaching, research, and service and means which might be used to assess these components. He would consistently refuse either to involve faculty in the personnel evaluation process or explain the basis for specific salary and promotion recommendations. He would insist upon his prerogative to make these decisions all the while that his faculty would be busy persuading the dean that a new chairman is desperately needed.

A wise chairman would involve his faculty, or at least a representative group of it, in the knotty value determinations upon which personnel evaluation is premised long before recommendations on individuals are required. Faculty would discuss and reach some agreement on difficult questions like: What role should student evaluations play in evaluation of teaching effectiveness? Is research and publication an expectation of all faculty in the department? Are service on a university committee and off-campus consulting legitimate service functions of faculty, and, if so, what relative weight should they be assigned? What means should be employed to evaluate publications and teaching? What weights or percentages should be assigned to teaching, scholarly productivity, and public service in faculty evaluation? Should these weights be uniform for all faculty in the department or should they vary by individual according to his assignment? These are only the gross questions. What might well emerge from extensive deliberations would be a listing of characteristics of the "excellent teacher," the "adequate teacher," the "ineffective teacher" with similar descriptive characteristics for the scholarly productivity and service functions of the professor. If recommendations in these areas were developed by a sub-group of the faculty, the chairman might well bring them to the whole faculty for discussion and adoption. The existence of college- or university-wide guidelines, of course, would facilitate the process.

Such a process of making values explicit greatly enhances the likelihood that a chairman's recommendation on salary increases, for example, will be acceptable to the faculty and accepted by central administration as reasonable and defensible. In fact, time spent in such prior faculty deliberations can yield handsome dividends in broad-based support in this sensitive and crucial area. Faculty, like other human beings, are more likely to view as "fair" that decision in which they have participated.

SECURING RESOURCES

Faculty expect administrators to secure the financial resources necessary to carry on the educational enterprise. The individual faculty member expects his chairman to fight for an adequate departmental budget. Chairman expect deans to allocate the resources necessary to support classes, faculty salary increases, professional travel, and the like. And everybody (students, faculty, chairmen, deans) expect the president to do battle as necessary with the external publics (boards, legislatures, governors, foundations, private donors, alumni) to secure an adequate institutional budget.

Most faculty could have cared less about the bureaucratic budget process in the 1950s and '60s. These were years of plenty for higher education, years when faculty salaries doubled, years of constantly expanding student enrollments and substantial annual incremental budget increases. Except for self-imposed limitations in a few institutions, the questions in most public colleges and universities were always: How many additional students this year? How many new faculty to be recruited and appointed? How many added dollars to allocate to new and expanded programs over last year?

A scarcity of qualified faculty meant that a good faculty member dissatisfied with his teaching load, compensation, or research support funds found his answer in professional mobility. If an associate professorship or a six-hour teaching load was not forthcoming at his own institution, there was always another eager to recruit talent and financially able to meet his requirements. In fact, a chairman and his senior faculty in many an American college and university in these two decades spent a sizable proportion of their time in recruiting able faculty from other institutions. Meanwhile graduate schools geared up to turn out ever more potential faculty to meet the apparently insatiable demands which the frequent doubling and tripling of student bodies, faculties, and resources implied.

The dawn of the 1970s lighted a different academic scene. Students, particularly undergraduates, became dissatisfied with mass production education, vaguely unhappy with faculty members more interested in research and publication for professional advancement than with teaching and advising. Legislators, reflecting a larger public attitude and confronted with very real increased demands for funds for all manner of public services such as welfare and highways, cast a more critical eye on appropriations for higher education. A governor of a large industrial state, for example, stated publicly that he had little difficulty in making a decision on where to effect needed cuts in the state's budget when forced to choose between the needs of children, mothers, and unemployed fathers dependent on welfare and higher education.

Even within higher education, dramatic shifts in where funds were allocated were becoming evident. Community and junior colleges would get more; senior institutions relatively less. Private colleges, many facing serious financial problems, would share in the more limited public resources. Aid would go in larger proportions more directly to students and therefore indirectly to the colleges and universities they chose to attend, partly as a response to the financial plight of the private institutions. Graduate programs, producing an apparent oversupply of doctorates, would be looked at most critically, with a moritorium on graduate program development not uncommon.

Budgets would be increased in much more modest proportions than earlier, or even decreased. Priorities would be established among public services with institutions of higher education competing on a more equal basis for budget allocations with mental health, highway construction, public welfare, and correctional institutions. Priorities would be established among and within institutions of higher education. Relatively stable institutional budgets would mean reduction of some educational programs, including reducing the number of faculty teaching in the program, and limited development of new programs accompanied by reduction in the old to accommodate the new programs. Fewer students —a totally new experience for many a college—translated to fewer dollars. And then faculty become vitally interested in the bureaucratic budgetary process they had long ignored.

The financial management task of the academic administrator also took a dramatic change of direction in the early 1970s. In the area of securing resources, it changed from the relatively easy job of totaling the new dollar requirements of added students, programs, and buildings. The process was incremental. That is, so many new students and new academic programs translated to so many additional dollars. Few were required to justify the "base budget"—what the institution had available the previous year. Less true in private than public institutions, the incremental or "add on" budget in the period of constant growth and expansion required only that the administrator justify the additions, rarely the base. In the area of allocating resources to program units, the task changed similarly. The change is best described by the introduction of program priorities and program budgeting.

Given fewer or the same dollars and the inflation factor (less real income), a college or university is faced with two alternatives. It can institute an across-the-board policy on budget allocation. In a stable situation, this might reveal itself in a decision, such as that made in California, to "freeze" faculty salaries at the previous year's level. Given fewer total dollars, it might mean a 5 or 10 percent reduction of the number of faculty employed applicable to every department and conditioned only by such factors as the number of temporary faculty in a particular department or the existence of a department where all faculty are tenured. An attractive first approach and an easy administrative solution, the across-the-board reduction is intellectually indefensible. High-quality academic programs for which there is significant student demand and societal need are harmed equally with mediocre, low-demand programs.

The more difficult alternative, of course, requires establishing program priorities. It requires answering very difficult questions like: What things are we now doing that are essential to the existence of a college or university? What activities do we now support that are desirable but not necessary? What criteria should be employed to judge which programs or activities should be given increased resources and which reduced support? Should some programs be eliminated to preserve quality in other programs? These are the new questions for the college administrator of the seventies. They are questions which should have been asked all along, but must be answered now by any institution aiming at anything but mediocrity. Given limited resources, no institution can do all things well. Rather, it must determine what it can do best and what it should not attempt to do at all, and then allocate its resources accordingly.

The able administrator will involve faculty and students in the intellectual challenge presented in establishment of program priorities. He will not expect that faculty, for example, will make the ultimate decisions on budget allocations to program units, but he will require participation in the process of establishing values upon which those allocations are premised. Questions such as the following are not matters for arbitrary administrative decision: What is the relative weight which should be assigned to existing faculty competence, student demand, and societal manpower need for academic programs? Are the service functions of an academic department (general education, providing courses to other majors) more or less important than the provision of courses for student majors in the discipline? What conditions characterize an academically excellent program as against an adequate or weak program? What should be the nature of the budget decision when an academically weak program is found to be essential to the mission of the institution? If a mediocre academic program is not essential to institutional goals, should it be eliminated or phased-out and, if so, what should happen to faculty teaching and students enrolled in the program?

Program budgeting presumes that these sorts of priority questions will be asked and answered about all programs each budget year. A program's budget, in other words, is justified from "scratch" each year. Justification is required for the program and its total budget request, not just for the additive portion of the request. Most attempts at programmatic budgeting in higher education, largely imposed by coordinating boards or budget bureau agencies, have been crude as they apply to existing programs rather than proposed additions of new programs. An academic administrator, however, may reasonably expect that the kind of justification now being required for approval of new graduate programs, will eventually be required, and within this decade, for every academic program. Those institutions and administrators who wait for external imposition will probably be both dissatisfied with the process employed and ill-prepared to meet the requirements of program budgeting. Securing adequate resources for his department, college, or university in the new era of financial stringency for higher education requires that the administrator understand and/or implement a programmatic approach to budgeting.

EFFECTIVE COMMUNICATION

Faculty require communicative skill in administrators. They expect educational leaders who are articulate spokesmen for faculty and institutional interests. Beyond this, they also desire administrative leadership capable of creating effective horizontal and vertical communication patterns. Good horizontal communication means effective communication from faculty to faculty, among students, from one administrator to another. Effective upward vertical communication—a very real need of faculty—implies largely passive communication skills of the administrator, such as openness and willingness to listen to faculty viewpoints on the part of a chairman or dean with some evidence of feedback. Downward vertical communication (dean to chairman, administrator to faculty, faculty to student) ordinarily requires a higher proportion of the more active communicative skills.

Brief contemplation of the amount of time an administrator spends listening, speaking, reading, and writing should convince even a skeptic that effective communication skills are critical administrative tools. An even closer examination of "communication time" reveals that the active skills of writing and speaking consume relatively more time of the leader than the more passive activities of reading and listening. A student is likely to spend the bulk of his time reading assigned materials and listening to his professor's lecture. A faculty member will spend proportionally more of his time talking to and with students and colleagues, and, particularly if he is an active scholar, in writing. A chairman or dean, while expected to read (professional articles and books, all manner of educational "literature" from department minutes to faculty reports to intra-institutional memoranda) and listen (student and faculty viewpoints, problems, expectations), spends progressively more time in the active role of speaker and writer. The higher the administrative role, the wider the audience and the more the total time devoted to communicative acts. One other observation is that the higher the administrative level, the larger the proportion of active communication devoted to external audiences such as board members, citizens, legislators, administrators of other institutions.

Unfortunately, some academic administrators are likely to dismiss concern with communication as fascination with "mere rhetoric" divorced from substance and reality. An early teacher, Aristotle, saw no such distinction between rhetoric (utilizing the available means of persuasion) and action. The university president who saw his request for a much-needed new $10-million science facility lost on a tie vote of a state board of higher education might have wondered if the need had been presented in the most persuasive manner possible, if the written justification contained the reality of need for the building, if fifteen minutes spent in conversation with a negatively inclined board member convincing him of the validity of the request might have made a significant difference in the quality of science education received by students at that president's university. Collective bargaining sessions between faculty organizations and administrative representatives — a more common phenomenon in American colleges — do result in very real conditions of actual contracts, conditions influenced heavily by the quality of argument and presentation in those sessions.

Faculty expect their administrators to be able communicators. In fact, they consistently include "ability to communicate effectively" among the criteria for administrative appointment. Many an administrator is recommended for appointment largely on the basis of both the substance of his thought and quality of his communicative ability as evidenced in interviews with faculty selection committees and administrators. Once in office, the more specific major communication skills expected of the administrator by faculty, in rough priority order, are:

1. Ability to articulate clearly and persuasively the goals and needs of the academic unit to students, other faculty and administrators, and external audiences.

2. Ability to discern faculty expectations to be communicated, largely through a willingness to listen to faculty, with some evidence that upward communication has impact.

3. Effective group communication leadership, including specific skills in small group discussion leadership, a knowledge of parliamentary procedure for more formal proceedings (including some departmental meetings), and a willingness to take the time needed to achieve, when possible, faculty consensus on controversial issues.

4. Effective articulation of informational requests and unit policy in clear, concise writing, often in memoranda to the faculty.

5. Knowledge of current concerns of the academic discipline or disciplines represented in the administrative unit as evidenced in a knowledge of the literature of the field(s).

6. Scholarly productivity on the part of the administrator through evidence of his own research and publication.

The priority notion here is intended to reveal that faculty will tolerate an administrator who is not an active scholar if he does an excellent job of articulating faculty needs, is willing to listen to faculty, and can preside intelligently over faculty deliberations. Faculty, on the other hand, are very likely to be super-critical of an administrator's lack of disciplinary knowledge or his lack of active scholarship when they are dissatisfied in one or a combination of the first four areas. A common complaint of administrators is that the demands imposed upon them in these four areas preclude their "keeping up" in their disciplines quite aside from active research and publication. This reality, perhaps unfortunately, often leads to a professional administration cadre.

PARTICIPATORY GOVERNANCE

The faculty claim to participation in college or university governance is rooted in the claim that teaching is a profession. The usual characteristics of a "profession" (for example, law, medicine) are extensive educational requirements, certified competence, control on new entrants into the profession, the existence of a self-imposed ethical code and disciplinary process, and a high degree of freedom in defining working conditions, frequently through self-employment.

College teaching meets most of these preconditions of professionalism. The standard certification for full-standing in the profession is the doctorate. Professors themselves do exercise effective control on who enters the profession by virtue of defining the educational requirements of the degree program, selecting degree candidates, and approving or disapproving the candidate's qualifying examination and dissertation. Both general and specific

discipline ethical codes exist with about the same low level of en-
forcement for violations as evident in other professions—that is,
only flagrant violations are subject to censure or expulsion. Tenure,
not self-employment, has provided the academic man relative freedom in definition of working conditions, particularly when coupled
with a high degree of professional mobility.

The competence argument—who but a physicist is qualified to
determine the nature of a physics curriculum, who but a physicist
is qualified to judge the quality of research and teaching in physics
—has yielded a high level of self-governance or at least shared
authority on campus, particularly in the vital areas of educational
programing and personnel evaluation. When the administration is
seen as the "enemy," it is most often because presidents and deans
tend to tamper with the assumption of faculty competence. Thus a
dean had best have very good reasons based on clearly defined
criteria for overriding the faculty promotion recommendation of a
departmental faculty; a president had best be prepared to accept
the curricular recommendations which filter up through the curriculum committee structure of his institution unless he has power-
fully persuasive arguments to the contrary. Any challenge in these
areas will be viewed by the faculty as arbitrary administration.

More recently, the challenge to faculty dominance has come
not from administration, but from students. The initial student
powerlessness reaction was directed against administration. A
dean's office would be occupied to express student discontent with
"factory education," uninterest of faculty in undergraduate students and teaching, and preoccupation of faculty with research and
off-campus consulting in many a prestigious university. Demands
would be presented to a president to institute a black studies program. Administrators, often powerless to act on such matters without faculty consent, turned teachers. The faculty, administrators
told students, exercises real authority to determine faculty rewards
and authorize new curricula. If students want to shape the direction
of higher education, they said, then students must not content
themselves with administrative attack but get involved in the process at the level where recommendations are formulated. To
achieve change, students would have to become members of departmental curriculum and personnel committees, college councils,
and academic senates.

Students, ultimately more interested in shaping the system to fit their needs than in destruction of the system, learned. Faculty in response warily agreed to increase the student voice in institutional governance. Student advisory committees in departments, voting student members of influential department and college educational policy committees, significant numbers of student members on what had traditionally been faculty senates became commonplace rather than the exception in the late sixties and early seventies. While faculty remained hard to convince that students had the competence which entitled them to participation in the inner-councils of the academy, they nevertheless largely acquiesced to vocal student demands for participatory governance. "Shared authority" on campus during this period extended from the traditional faculty-administration participation to faculty-student-administrative involvement. The effects of this change in academic governance remain to be determined, but there can be little doubt that increased student participation has meant decreased faculty influence. One result may well be increased authority by administrators and governing boards, particularly in areas of disagreement between students and faculty.

Another undetermined factor is the effect of faculty unionization for collective bargaining — most faculty unionizers prefer the term "professional negotiations" to collective bargaining. The existence of a faculty bargaining unit and a contract, of course, transfers much of the effective power from the small college faculty meeting or college/university senate to the bargaining table and negotiations between administrators and faculty union representatives. Students are largely excluded; whether legitimate student interests are excluded remains to be seen. Still largely a phenomenon at public institutions in urban-industrial states, faculty collective bargaining, if it increases as most administrators expect it to increase, will modify significantly the way in which faculty participate. The definitive studies on how the faculty and the administrative roles are modified remain to be completed.

Another powerful factor has operated in recent years to diminish the faculty role in institutional decision-making. The existence and authority of statewide higher education coordinating commissions and boards, such as the Illinois Board of Higher Education, have eroded institutional autonomy. To the degree that these statewide agencies have authority to approve academic programs and institutional budgets, they exercise effective control of institutional (including faculty) ambitions. Created to rationalize planning and the allocation of resources and control costs, these agencies have created considerable bureaucracies for centralized decision-making, resulting in a concomitant loss of authority by local administration (including presidents) and faculty. The trend is sketched in Newman's *Report on Higher Education*, which concludes that "the flexibility, differentiation, and individual responsiveness" of colleges and universities "are slipping away" and "only a determined effort can revise this trend."[5]

Increased student participation in institutional governance and the rapid increase in statewide coordination, particularly in the public sector, have diminished the effective authority of faculty in establishing educational policy. This has been a major factor in the faculty decision to turn to professional negotiations as an alternative to more traditional forms of faculty participation in governance. Faculty expectations of administration will change accordingly if this trend persists.

PROTECTION FROM EXTERNAL THREATS

Administrators are expected by faculty to provide a buffer against external threats of two kinds, threats to academic freedom and threats to employment security. These faculty expectations have been linked together in the most basic faculty value of academic freedom and tenure. The rationale for linking the two concepts together includes:

1. The essential functions of the professor, communication and extension of knowledge, can only be performed effectively in an atmosphere where the teacher is free to inquire into and then "profess" what he believes to be true. The ultimate test of "truth" is the marketplace of ideas, not the immediate public acceptability of a particular fact, theory, or point of view.

2. Society benefits from the free exchange of ideas; it stagnates where unpopular thought is repressed. The professor must be free to analyze and criticize the political, economic, social institutions

of the society—even its philosophical and moral underpinnings—if knowledge is to be brought to bear on improvement of the human condition. A society unwilling to tolerate and even support academic critics will succumb to a dogma untested by rational discourse.

3. The college teaching profession must provide a sufficient degree of economic security to attract competent men and women. While professors seem not to expect income levels comparable to business and industry, they should have sufficient compensation to guarantee intellectual independence and certainly enough to allow them to focus on inquiry and teaching without concern for basic needs for themselves and their families.

4. Adequate compensation must be coupled with job security, which is provided through the tenure system, for the profession to be attractive to able persons. Properly conceived, academic tenure is a sophisticated form of due process providing that, after a trial period extending not more than seven years, a professor may be dismissed only for incompetence or other just cause and then only when the basis for dismissal is confirmed by professional colleagues. Anything less is not only unprofessional but subjects the professor to economic and political pressures harmful to both the professor and the society.

Administrators have been expected to accept and defend this rationale, to secure the resources necessary for adequate faculty compensation, to defend the academic freedom of faculty against generalized public attack and misunderstanding, and to assure due process (colleague judgment) in individual faculty academic freedom and tenure cases. Thus, a complete familiarity with academic freedom and tenure standards of the profession is a requirement of the academic administrator.[6]

The nature of this traditional expectation, however, is changing radically with the expansion of professional negotiations in higher education. Partly as a result of what faculty perceive to be an inadequate defense and implementation of the academic freedom and tenure concept, including most recently the failure of faculty salary increases to keep pace with the cost of living, faculty power is being utilized to formalize in collective bargaining agreements what had previously been simply accepted practice, sometimes embodied in institutional governance documents.

Presidents and their boards, many faculty argue, have not always enthusiastically supported academic freedom and tenure concepts, have sometimes seemed to utilize financial difficulty to rid the faculty of what they consider to be undesirable elements, and have failed to generate the public support necessary to provide resources needed for adequate compensation of faculty. Knowledge of the success of the collective bargaining model in other segments of society (including in the public schools) has led an increasing proportion of faculty to seek more positive responses through unionization. If administration proves inadequate in protecting faculty from external threats, collective bargaining advocates claim, then the answer must be found in negotiated contracts.

The existence of a contract in a college or university alters radically administrative expectation. The dean and president, long viewed as colleagues rather than management, now become adversaries at the bargaining table. Less certain is the role of department chairmen, who are sometimes included and sometimes excluded from the faculty bargaining unit. Administrators in contract institutions, however, tend to assume much more clearly a management perspective and role expectation. The administrators or the administrative bargaining team is now on the opposite side of the table from faculty, sharpening the division between the faculty and the administrative faculty member.

Many questions remain unanswered without further experience with professional negotiations. Will faculty continue to view administrators as responsible for protecting faculty from external threats or will administrators themselves be perceived as part of the external threat? Will the concept of shared authority (faculty participation in internal governance) survive collective bargaining or will it simply be written into the contracts? Can negotiations be limited to direct economic issues (compensation level, definition of faculty work load), or will they extend to include matters such as academic freedom, definition of faculty-administrator relations, governance systems, student-faculty relations, degree requirements —every aspect of the higher education enterprise? An examination of several actual contracts provide good reason to expect the latter.

EFFICIENT HANDLING OF ROUTINE OPERATIONS

A final faculty expectation of the administration is the efficient handling of routine organizational matters, especially personnel and work assignments. Among the characteristics of an efficient academic administrator are:

1. *Providing equitable work assignments.* A chairman, for example, must allocate teaching loads in such a fashion that faculty feel their talents and expertise are being best utilized, that numbers of preparations as well as numbers of students and difficulty of task (large classes versus small classes, undergraduate versus graduate courses, new versus familiar instructional assignments) are taken into account. It is also expected that, where appropriate, allowance for faculty research and service as well as teaching expectations are considered.

2. *Processing routine communications.* Handling regular mail and telephone business of the academic unit with reasonable dispatch consumes a sizable amount of any administrator's time. Faculty generally have little appreciation or even respect for such routine administrative requirements but do expect prompt response to their own administrative inquiries. The administrator who fails to develop an efficient routine for responding to phone calls, dictating or drafting correspondence, and filing information for ready reference will soon find himself immersed in a sea of paper. Two things are essential: (1) very able secretarial assistance and (2) a routine for handling office communications that allows sufficient time for thinking on implementation of more long-range goals.

3. *Providing needed information and support services for unit personnel.* The departmental chairman who neglects to inform his faculty of when sabbatical leave requests or research applications must be submitted or who cannot secure resources needed to type and reproduce examinations will find his faculty seeking a new chairman. Faculty will scoff at this "paper clip counting" role of the administrator at the same time they fully expect paper clips, telephone service, secretarial assistance, audiovisual equipment needed for classes, computer cards needed for research, and all of the other paraphernalia of academic support for faculty to be readily available. The administrator had best be able to either provide it or (second best) provide information on how and where to obtain it.

4. *Scheduling necessary meetings.* Faculty expect both that the administrator will not bother them with unnecessary meetings and that the administrator will involve them in discussion of departmental affairs. This requires dissemination of routine information by memoranda, judgment about when an issue requires faculty discussion, and efficient presentation of issues and handling of discussion when faculty do meet.

5. *Providing required unit reports.* Any complex human organization requires periodic informational reports for efficient management. Enrollment, personnel, budget, curriculum reports, among others, must be processed. An annual department report summarizing faculty accomplishments, student enrollments, program improvement, and similar items is not an uncommon expectation of the chairman. Faculty expect to be well represented in such institutional documents, but they also expect the administrator to meet such bureaucratic requirements while they spend their own time on teaching and scholarly productivity.

6. *Creating effective interpersonal relationships.* A final time-consuming requirement of any administrative officer from chairman to president is creating a climate of good interpersonal relationships within the academic unit. This may require precious hours in listening to professional and even personal problems of academic staff and trying, where possible, to do something about these problems. The recognition that unit morale affects unit productivity justifies this energy expenditure.

SUMMARY

When faculty set forth criteria for administrative appointment, they come forth with a set of expectations few human beings can fulfill. They want a great teacher who is also a nationally recognized scholar in his discipline with demonstrated administrative capacity. They want leadership within the context of democratic values, including significant faculty (and to a lesser extent, student) involvement. They want an Academic Superman.

Willing to temper idealism with reality, what faculty insist upon from on-the-job administrators includes evidence of: (1) educational leadership which tempers a clear concept of what is required to improve the quality of education with faculty judgments on the matter; (2) the ability to make fair, reasonable decisions, certainly the ability to make decisions; (3) the ability to secure the budgetary resources needed to carry on a quality program; (4) the capacity to communicate efficiently and effectively, including a willingness to listen to the views of others as well as speak well; (5) the ability to work for and within a participatory governance structure; (6) the willingness and ability to defend faculty interests in the areas of academic freedom and employment security; and (7) the capacity to handle the organizational routine efficiently and in such a fashion as to allow faculty to concentrate on teaching and scholarly productivity. While these administrative expectations do not vary significantly by level (chairman, dean, president), they are being conditioned significantly at present by the increase of collective bargaining, relatively modest financial support for higher education, and a significant decrease in the mobility of faculty.

NOTES

1. This categorization is based partly on intensive discussions with several faculty members on what they expect of their administrators. While no quantitative approach was attempted, each category in the listing was mentioned by more than one of the faculty members interviewed. It is also evident that categories overlap; they are viewed as discrete here only for purposes of analysis and description.

2. This listing of presidential functions is typical of many. See, for example: State of Illinois *Governing Policy for the Regency Universities.*

3. Carnegie Commission on Higher Education, *Reform on Campus: Changing Students, Changing Academic Programs,* June, 1972. The finding is based on a survey of 60,000 faculty members. The findings are fairly consistent, also, by type of institution— graduate-research universities, liberal arts colleges, and two-year institutions.

4. *Reform on Campus,* pp. 76-77.

5. Task Force on Higher Education (Frank Newman, chairman), Department of Health, Education, and Welfare, *Report on Higher Education,* March, 1971, p. 27.

6. A thorough treatment is provided in the American Association of University Professors' publication, *Academic Freedom and Tenure*.

SUPPLEMENTARY REFERENCES

ABBOTT, FRANK C. *Faculty-Administration Relationships*. Washington: American Council on Education, 1958.

BUDIG, GENE A. *Perceptions in Public Higher Education*. Lincoln: University of Nebraska Press, 1970.

DYKES, ARCHIE R. *Faculty Participation in Academic Decision Making*. Washington: American Council on Education, 1968.

EURICH, ALVIN C. *Campus 1980: The Shape of the Future in Higher Education*. New York: Academy for Educational Development, 1969.

HEFFERLIN, J. B. LON, and ELLIS L. PHILLIPS. *Information Services for Academic Administration*. San Francisco: Jossey-Bass, Inc., 1971.

JOUGHIN, LOUIS (ed.). *Academic Freedom and Tenure: A Handbook of the American Association of University Professors*. Madison: University of Wisconsin Press, 1967.

KEETON, MORRIS. *Shared Authority on Campus*. Washington: American Association for Higher Education, 1971.

CHAPTER 3

What the Trustee Expects

Ten years ago college and university trustees generally made few excessive demands on their academic administrators. They tended to assume that their professional staff members would:

1. Do a consistently competent job of administering, thus requiring only token review by the governing board;
2. Alert them of any sensitive issues which might focus unfavorable public attention on the campus and the trustees;
3. Speak effectively for the governing board on matters of institutional policy;
4. Bear the burden of public criticism for the total academic community.

In a sense, college and university trustees of that era were really absentee landlords who preferred to employ hired hands for purposes other than ceremonial ones. It is important to point out that ten years ago many leading citizens aspired to membership on governing boards. This is not so today. Governors, who in a number of instances make trustee appointments, report that it is "most difficult" to interest qualified persons in such assignments.[1] Leading citizens simply do not want to take the pressure involved and they no longer believe that an association with higher education is highly attractive.

One needs to remember that historically governing boards have been regarded as places to reward the community's elite, the community's successful. They were thought to be positions in which one could render non-controversial, gentlemanly public service. They were not bodies that concerned themselves with explosive issues. They were isolated and, in part, enshrined.

Traditional views of the trusteeship have been shattered in the aftermath of campus disruption and student unrest, and resulting trustee expectations of college administrators have multiplied many times over.[2] An increasing number of college presidents believe the situation has reached a point where they no longer can be effective as administrators because of unrealistic trustee demands on their time, and they see no relief in the near future, realizing that today's governing board member finds himself cast into a swirling sea of controversy. The outlook is for more of the same—considerable heat, considerable pressure. Trustees in higher education are very much aware of this, and they rightfully look to the future with uncertainty and apprehension. They realize that governing boards, in both public and private institutions, will be likely targets for greatly intensified attacks by student, faculty, and public pressure groups. They are looking to their administrators for some understanding and considerable protection.

THE STUDENT ROLE

Students are likely to be the most aggressive. They are eager to train their sights on the often exposed flank of the trustee. They regard their institutional board members as deserving of fire.[3] It is significant to note that many trustees are convinced that their administrative officers have not tried hard enough to protect them from student criticism. Some believe that their administrators, and especially their presidents, have straddled the fence, using the governing board as a protective wedge. One source of irritation for trustees is the administrative response to students that governing boards make institutional policy and the administrator *only* carries it out. Members of governing boards now claim to have been burned by administrators who propose policies, advocate their adoption, and disavow the ramifications. They argue that administrators are well compensated and as their staff officers should lead both the offense in supporting institutional policy and the defense in blunting harsh student reaction of it.

In recent years, student militants have painted the trustees as "tools of the establishment," representatives of a self-serving, status quo social order. "They—the trustees—represent what we are trying to overturn" declared a University of Wisconsin student leader during one of the Madison campus upheavals. This is a common expression among the more liberal students. What offends countless governing board members is that the militants have been most effective in typing them, and the trustees feel wronged. They seem to be venting their frustrations on their employees, the administrators of higher education, resulting in a noticeably strained relationship between the trustee and the administrator.

Significantly, most of the vocal student leaders have taken hostile exception to the composition of governing boards, capitalizing on the fact that many of them are controlled by the economically successful and the socially acceptable. Some educational observers—including trustees—believe that the militants have touched upon a sensitive nerve in higher education, one that might, if skillfully exploited, attract considerable support from the previously uncommitted students. Militant appeals are being made, and will continue to be made, on the basis of equal representation.

Trustees on certain campuses which have experienced student turmoil have been branded as dictators—absolute rulers who permit no meaningful student participation in major issues of self-determination on the campus, such as rules and regulations governing out-of-class behavior. In some student quarters, the trustees have been depicted as individuals who do not comprehend higher learning and who do not have enough reverence for the principles of academic freedom and individual growth. Channels of communication between trustees and students never have been too effective, largely because governing boards seldom took students seriously until recent times, and students rarely had the inclination to approach trustees on substantive matters. One can safely state that both sides were mutually uninterested in each other until the mid-1960s. This is no longer the case. Both students and trustees are insisting upon improved communication, but sometimes for different reasons. Often caught in the middle is the administrator who is expected to originate informational meetings, preside over them, and mediate between the two sides, often on philosophically irreconcilable differences.

BOARDS ARE SKEWED

National studies, in recent years, have confirmed that governing boards are skewed in favor of individuals with economic means. Membership is also skewed in favor of older persons, a fact which has served as an irritant to the youthful campus liberals.

Briefly, the militants base their case against the trustees on these points:

1. Large segments of the general citizenry are not represented on governing boards, while they are being required to shoulder part of the economic burden of higher learning.

2. Politically potent sectors of the American society, such as organized labor, women, and the lower socio-classes, are not well represented on the existing governing boards.

3. Most of the trustees are older—between fifty and fifty-five years of age—and politically conservative, which means, according to current student concepts, they are unable to provide enlightened leadership for the collegiate community.

4. Relatively few trustees are willing or able to bridge the so-called generation gap.

These issues generally have met with enthusiasm among liberal students, especially those who are continually in search of campus issues which might gather broader-based peer support. Leaders of the more liberal student organizations have not limited their support of these issues to the campus. They have worked long hours in trying to sell point two to the blue-collar worker and to the black. They contend that this is one issue on which organized labor and the black can unite. There are increasing signs that labor, especially in the very large metropolitan areas, has taken the bait, now insisting that it does have a vested interest in the direction and management of American higher education. Labor is organizing its political machine to assure greater representation on governing boards, especially in the area of public higher education. There are some signs that the blacks plan a united campaign to claim more trusteeships.

According to certain student leaders, the representation issue in higher education will be alive and explosive for at least the next ten years. They believe it will be the basis of many, many on- and off-campus confrontations. It is an American issue, they reason, with universal appeal.

Those students most intent on stirring campus emotions tend to regard administrators as secondary targets, largely because official policy-making powers rest with the governing board, not the administration. They see administrators as captive subordinates, not insensitive instigators. They see trustees at the root of major problems and administrators as mere props with high visibility. It should be noted that some student liberals have been frustrated with college administrators, finding them outwardly well-meaning and often verbally elusive.

It is likely that student representation on governing boards of colleges and universities, initiated at the University of Kentucky in 1968, will grow during the next ten-year period. Boards of trustees at the Universities of Connecticut and Maine have student members with voting rights. These student trustees are appointed by the governors. Massachusetts, in 1969, became the first state to pass a law giving students a voting membership on state college and university governing boards, including the board of the University of Massachusetts.

Despite these and other imposing inroads by students, the militants still talk of "tokenism — more of the same." Their expressed aim, although totally unrealistic with public opinion being what it is today, is control of the governing boards, absolute authority over all matters that pertain to student life and activities on the campus. They admit to wanting "a sanctuary from the establishment." Considerable trustee blame for these student illusions of grandeur has been laid at the door of the administration. There are governing boards which have dismissed administrative officers because of an apparent unwillingness to take more rigid stands with students on governance issues. One may be assured that college administrators will be expected to draw much harder lines with students in the years ahead.

THE FACULTY INTEREST

Serving to heighten the anxiety of trustees is the fact that certain elements within the college and university faculties have sided with the students on a number of the previously cited issues, giving active encouragement from time to time. The American Association of University Professors, on several occasions, cited the representation issue in public discussions. Their position has been compatible with the one expressed by the student liberals. It should be pointed out that some governing board members suspect collusion between the faculty and the administration.

Many trustees contend that the faculties will be lining up opposite them in the years ahead. They look for faculty members to push for representation on the governing boards. Faculty members have presented this issue in the past, reasoning that they, as professionals, know more about higher education than lay representatives. They have asked for a greater voice in the maintenance and development of the educational program and institution.

For years the AAUP has been expressing concern about the trustees' understanding and appreciation for academic standards and academic freedom. In some instances their concern has been rewarded with more direct participation with trustees in institutional deliberations, but not too often in formal representation or in voting power. The opposing forces cite the advantages of having trustees who are personally free from direct institutional involvement, who can look at the academy and its problems with objectivity. Involved faculty members, they reason, cannot provide such a dispassionate analysis.

Debate revolving around the issue of faculty representation on governing boards infrequently includes college and university administrators. They prefer to remain mute, realizing the likelihood of being caught between two very diverse constituencies. When pressed into taking a position, a majority of the administrators will offer passive support to their employers, the trustees, while acknowledging the virtue of faculty declarations.[4]

Those who have studied the issue of faculty representation on governing boards generally believe that there is a reasonable compromise, one that would give the professional educator a place on the board. But they say that since the board of trustees represents the public interest, it seems wise to assure that lay members retain the majority. Such a compromise appears likely to be implemented rather widely in the next decade in both public and private institutions. Trustees freely acknowledge that they will need faculty support in the trying days ahead, and faculty members believe that they will have to be better represented in the development of institutional policies, especially those that affect the academic program.

What concerns many trustees is the possibility of a student-faculty coalition, designed to usurp the powers of the governing board and the campus administration. For this reason, trustees have been more receptive to discussion of the representation issue with both students and faculty members in the last five years. Trustee expectations of the administration on the matter are unmistakable — they expect their administrators to administer, not to politic. They in no way want the administration involved, believing this to be an issue on which they must cast their own ballots. They question whether anyone is able or willing to state their case as they think it should be presented.

There can be little doubt that broader representation on the governing boards would be advantageous to all of higher education. One needs to be aware of the obvious disparities. For example, nearly 70 percent of the trusteeships are held by business and professional people. Fewer than 10 percent are women. Most simply stated, trusteeships in American higher education have gone to individuals who have resources, time, and prestige. Organized labor and the blacks have held only token representation.

Some researchers, including Hubert Beck, propose the use of a principle of broad representation. For example, they favor *public* representation from business, the professions, agriculture and labor; they favor *institutional* representation from alumni, faculty, and students.

THE TRUSTEE'S SIDE

To really understand what motivates trustees and prompts their newfound expectations of the administration, one needs to realize that in the past five years governing board members have felt intense pressure and criticism from the general public too.[5] They have been rapped — and repeatedly — for institutional turmoil caused by student and faculty dissatisfaction. It is essential to point out that most citizens initially laid the blame for campus disruptions at the door of the campus president and his staff. Today the blame is *shared* with the trustees, who legally, as a governing board, have the full authority and responsibility for the institution; there is no way in which the board can avoid its charge. It is true that trustees have traditionally delegated large areas of authority, but today they are more sensitive and restrictive about this delegation. They realize that they are legally, morally, and politically accountable. Innumerable trustees admit to feelings of deep frustration and growing cynicism, finding their governing roles uncomfortable and their administrative staffs unresponsive. They believe that they are shouldering an inordinate amount of the "shared" criticism for the academy. They are searching for what some term a "more equitable distribution" of accountability.

There is widespread agreement that college and university trustees will be thrust into the forefront of public attention and public scrutiny in the next ten years; they will be asked to stand up and be counted on highly explosive issues on which the citizenry will have strong and divided opinions. Governing board members will be expected to have innards of cast iron. Their positions are not likely to be political springboards or socially rewarding memberships. Their positions will be lively seats of controversy.

In many ways it is tragic that today's trustees are being so besieged with criticism, for never have their roles been so important; never have their responsibilities been so great; and never have administrative expectations of them been so high. It is essential to acknowledge that college and university presidents, from both public and private institutions, will direly need trustee support during the 1970s. One must face the fact that higher education is suspect in many public quarters. It desperately needs sympathetic and articulate lay board members to forge the way with the general public; without them and their active assistance, efforts of college and university administrators to win public confidence and needed financial support will be crippled seriously.

According to representative collegiate administrators, trustees generally have been:

Highly effective in working with the president and his staff for adequate state legislative appropriations. They — the trustees — have been utilized to explain the educational program and its financial needs in "layman terms" to the usually cautious state legislators.

Most successful in maintaining alumni support for the educational programs in spite of adverse publicity resulting from campus disruptions. Much of their work for the private institutions has been accomplished on a face-to-face basis, requiring inordinate amounts of time and personal sacrifice.

Criticized for performing the tasks that the campus administration wanted them to do, namely those of raising funds and supporting the institutional budget. It is true that board members most often are people of influence; and it is also true that collegiate administrators attempt to translate this "influence" into dollars for educational programing.

Tagged to serve as "whipping posts" for the more radical elements within the academic community.

It is safe to assume that college and university officials will be attempting to call upon their trustees for more and varied assistance in the years ahead. Helping to make budget presentations and offer plausible justifications should be standard concerns and areas of involvement for the governing board of the 1970s, many administrators believe.

SUMMARY

In summary, the historical relationship between the trustee and the college and university administrator has been amiable and productive. The trustee has assumed competence and the administrator has assumed trust.

Then came the turbulent days of campus upheaval when governing board members found themselves serving as targets for student, faculty, and public abuse. Much of that abuse was not warranted, but it left deep scars. Many trustees first were confused and later bitter.

They chose to strike out in a number of directions, but with special force at the campus administration. They felt alone; they believed the administration had deserted them by not shielding them from more of the controversy and criticism.

It is important to note that the administrator had genuine sympathy for the position of the trustees, but he found himself caught hopelessly among diverse institutional forces. His inaction was read by certain trustees as a sign of disloyalty. He often was typed as being either pro-student or pro-faculty when it came to the crucial issues on which trustees felt pressure and wanted support.

As the relationship deteriorated, trustee demands on the administrator became both excessive and abusive. What most knowing college and university officials desperately want today is an improved relationship with their governing boards. They want a productive association with trustees, realizing that without their steadfast backing true public support is not a possibility. They see the governing board as the primary key in unlocking essential support from agencies such as state and federal government.

One may be certain that the college and university administrator of the 1970s will be attempting to court his governing board, but it will require excessive persistence and patience. True reconciliation will not come easy. A return to the "good old days" appears quite remote, but not impossible.

NOTES

1. Thirty-four of the nation's governors participated in an educational survey conducted by Dr. Budig in the spring of 1971. Six of the twelve major questions dealt with college and university trustees. It should be noted that the governors thought it was "even more difficult" to get qualified people interested in seeking public election to institutional governing boards.

2. Interview with Dr. Logan Wilson, past president of the American Council on Education, October 9, 1970.

3. One hundred student government leaders from fifty colleges and universities participated in a study conducted by Dr. Budig in the spring of 1972. Questions centered on student attitudes on a variety of campus issues.

4. Seventy-five college and university presidents participated in an educational survey conducted by the president's office of the University of Nebraska in the winter of 1971.

5. Two hundred members of college and university governing boards participated in a study conducted by Dr. Budig in the summer of 1972.

SUPPLEMENTARY REFERENCES

BECK, HUBERT PARK. *Men Who Control Our Universities*. New York: King's Crown Press, 1947.

HENDERSON, ALGO D. *The Role of the Governing Board*. Washington: Association of Governing Boards of Universities and Colleges, 1967.

HUGHES, RAYMOND M. *A Manual for Trustees of Colleges and Universities*. Ames: Iowa State College Press, 1951.

RAUH, MORTON A. *The Trustees of Higher Education*. Washington: Association of Governing Boards of Universities and Colleges, 1969.

ZWINGLE, J. L. *The Lay Governing Board*. Washington: American Council on Education, 1970.

CHAPTER 4

Governmental and Public Expectations

Traditionally governors and state legislators have thought college and university administrators to be ineffective in communicating with the general public. They still do today. According to prevailing political view, academic administrators tend to:

1. Converse with the citizenry only when their institutions need financial assistance;
2. Take expressed public sentiment too lightly;
3. Regard citizens who question the objectives and practices of higher education as ill-advised enemies;
4. Assume that the citizenry owes them and their programs unyielding support;
5. Presume that the public knows about and appreciates what the academy is doing.[1]

There is consensus within the various state houses that college and university officers must alter appreciably their approach to the taxpayer by listening more and demanding less. If the politicians had their way, administrators would spend more time reaching out to the people, trying to learn what the institutions of higher learning might do to better serve local communities. One specific area in which many elected state officials believe higher education must make a greater contribution is adult and continuing education. This area clearly offers tangible possibilities for taking the educational strength of the academic community to the people, and thus diminishing the not unreal threat of intellectual isolationism. Certain knowledgeable observers, including Dr. Clark Keer, feel many of higher education's recent troubles could have been averted with broader-based, public support which is a by-product of relevant programing, both on and off the campus.

What rankles a number of governors and legislators most is the rather common practice among college and university presidents to deploy campus forces at budget time to persuade the electorate of the virtues of higher education and the need of elected officials to support it. In recent years these tactics have produced considerably more hostility than support among state politicians who regard them as blatant propaganda and not legitimate education. These same politicians question the propriety of using faculty and administrative staff for the purpose of lobbying citizens and pressuring legislators.

There is sensitivity on what constitutes legitimate support for higher education. Most state officials, for example, regard themselves as reasonable supporters of the academy, but not as blind supporters like a number of their predecessors were ten years ago. Academics consider them something far less.

It is reasonable to assume that academia will continue to find itself amid troubled waters, with more and more state officeholders seeming to delight in oration over what is wrong with higher education. They appear most receptive to corrective measures which are punitive in nature. They also seem to resent academics who talk back or respond harshly to their assertions. The more critical governors and legislators depict academic officers and faculty members as individuals who have had their own way for too long and who are unwilling to face salient criticism. These elected officials further claim to be representing a frustrated constituency which has had little, if any, real input into the determination of educational policy.

One should realize that certain influential politicians contend, and have been successful in convincing numerous citizens, that the institutions of higher learning are the captives of academics who operate the campus as a closed corporation under the guise of academic freedom and due process. Meaningful public inquiry and public participation, the politicians argue, are discouraged and true academic power is held by a few at the expense of many.

SPHERE OF POLITICAL REALITY

In reality growing numbers of state officeholders are typing the collegiate administrator as naive. They especially resent naivete when it appears coupled with outward obstinacy. They admit to being antagonized by what they perceive as official higher education's unwillingness to work within the sphere of political reality. Unfortunately, some college and university presidents have not been judicious in their requests to governors and state legislators in the past decade. They have asked for astronomical increases in their budgets while providing only minimal supporting data. They have rested their cases on the basic premise that higher education is good and people who question any aspects of it are bad. Quite frankly, they have regarded their budgets and educational philosophies as beyond public reproach.

Such an attitude is both presumptuous and passé. The immediate years ahead will demand college and university presidents who welcome questions about their budgets and operations; in fact, the astute administrators will be actively encouraging public inquiry, equating effective justification of their activities with institutional strength and well-being.

College administrators are learning that state legislatures are no longer dominated by individuals preoccupied with the affairs of rural America. Reapportionment has triggered dramatic change in legislative composition, interests, and priorities. Present emphasis is clearly focused on the areas of urban concern and involvement. It is significant to note that major state universities, for years deeply involved in agricultural research and planning, have lost at least some of their advantage before appropriation committees. Political power is where the voters are, and the voters are, and will continue to be, in urban settings.

During the last ten years, reapportionment evoking the one-man, one-vote concept has brought to the membership of state legislatures an ever-increasing number of people who are well informed about the problems of higher education because they themselves have experienced college and have sons and daughters who are participants in higher education. In some states the number of college graduates serving in legislative bodies has increased by more than a third.

College administrators are learning quickly, and rather painfully, that better educated legislators are not necessarily champions of increased financial support for education. In some instances they have proven themselves hostile and have used their learning to analyze most critically the proposals of a variety of governmental agencies, especially the public colleges and universities.

PREREQUISITES TO STRATEGY

To chart effective institutional strategies, the college and university president and his administrative associates need to have a bearing on which branch of state government is likely to be most supportive of higher education in the immediate years ahead. They need to sense where the real balance of power lies. They also need to understand how to approach this highly sensitive and politically dangerous situation.

To be sure, political considerations are among the most searching issues confronting today's academic administrator, and therein rests the essentials of whether academia will experience feast or famine. Although it is dangerous to generalize—and especially when the generalizations involve politicians and their actions—one can argue convincingly that, in the last ten years or so, governors have been more receptive than legislators to the legitimate needs of higher education.

Collegiate administrators find it easier to educate one governor than to reach sometimes hundreds of legislators with varying degrees of interest and receptivity. Thus, they have devoted appreciably more time to cultivating governors than legislators in recent years. The wisdom of such an approach is debatable. One also should realize that state legislators, as a group, tend to be more cautious or conservative than governors because they have to go home or back to their constituents at regular intervals. Their legislative jobs are not full-time and they do not enjoy the luxury of isolation as some occupants of executive mansions do.

The knowing president will maintain open communications with the governor and selected legislative leaders, such as standing committee chairmen, ever mindful of the chief executive's power of budgetary recommendation and veto and the legislature's ultimate power of appropriation. Serious students of state government generally believe that the executive branch will remain somewhat more receptive than the legislative branch to the impending needs of higher education. They also feel that the governor will retain a perilous edge in influence over the legislature which has taken bold strides to narrow this important gap in recent years. It should be pointed out that, in the last three to five years, numerous state legislators have voted themselves additional staff assistance, while paring, when and where possible, gubernatorial requests for increased staff support. Certain legislators argue that the balance of power is at issue, and they ascribe to a rigid principle of shared responsibility and shared power. For the past twenty years, they contend, the legislative branch of state government has abrogated, and the executive branch has dominated.

In the days, months, and years ahead, the college president should be careful not to alienate either the governor or the legislator because the scale of power in state government is tipped easily, and the academic administrator cannot afford to be cast on any one side, let alone on the losing one. Enrichment of the academic program—a prime objective of any quality institution of higher learning—is at stake.

A REPRESENTATIVE PUBLIC VIEW

During their torrid campaign for the Presidency in 1960, John F. Kennedy and Richard M. Nixon agreed that the city of Chicago was instrumental to their strategies for eventual success at the ballot box. Perhaps Mr. Kennedy said it best when he declared: "No candidate for President of the United States can win without an understanding of what the people of Chicago think and why. They are not only representative of the Midwest, but also of the other major population centers." Mr. Nixon said that Chicago offers "a unique and comprehensive cross section of American life. Its influence is staggering."[2]

Since that historic campaign of 1960, the city of Chicago has continued to grow in numbers of people and in political import, with the *New York Times* claiming "it is the beachhead of American political power." Therefore, the authors of this volume thought it wise to offer advice to college and university administrators *after* sampling the opinion of 200 representative Chicago residents on a number of highly significant educational issues.[3] They were asked:

1. *How important is a college education today?*

Their answers reflected considerable uncertainty, growing hostility, and genuine concern. Nearly half of the people questioned whether a college diploma was essential to economic success in today's setting; ten years ago, they said, the degree was a viable indicator of occupational success. In their opinion, colleges and universities have been preoccupied with growth for reasons of personal and institutional prestige, and have given little, if any, rational thought to basic matters of supply and demand. More than 60 percent of the respondents believe that most of the blame rests with the administrator whom they regard as a polished politician, and one who has misspent public trust. They perceive the administrator as an aloof dispenser of the tax monies who spends little time with matters of accountability. Forty percent of the people said that they wanted to believe in higher education but expressed reservation about its present scope and mission. They want greater emphasis on programs which come to grips with the politically sensitive issues of employability. They want a program of higher education which instantly produces economic and social assets, not directionless liabilities.

2. *Is higher education being adequately financed?*

Response to this question left little room for interpretation, with 192 of the 200 people saying yes, 5 saying no, and 3 voicing no opinion. According to the majority view, today's colleges and universities are administered by men and women who are either unwilling or incapable of taking hard positions on fiscal matters and bringing about needed program and operational changes. If appropriately redistributed, they believe, resources for higher education would be more than adequate for academic reform and program excellence. Three-fourths of the participants favor a reallocation of institutional funds, with priority given to efforts concerned with classroom innovation. Significantly, they appeared convinced that many young people are being turned off by the staid nature of the collegiate experience and are leaving the campus with little more than an intangible collection of academic credits. Certain state coordinating agencies, including the Illinois Board of

Higher Education, have suggested that the institutions initiate new programs *only* with funds resulting from internal reallocations of 2 to 3 percent. Countless state legislators like the idea and are destined to support it publicly. Even the United States Office of Education has encouraged the reallocation approach if the freed dollars can be channeled into programs favoring educational innovation and vocational opportunity.[4] Response from academia has been guarded. One must acknowledge that collegiate administrators, as a fraternity, were considerably more proficient in addition than subtraction throughout the generally bountiful 1960s. Until the early 1970s, true elimination of academic programs and services was rare; addition and enrichment of programs were the accustomed practice. It is significant to note that 169 of the respondents were convinced that the higher education community could reduce its economic base and scope of activity without impairing relevant program quality and development.

3. How should colleges and universities be changed?

Their curricular options should be studied, revised, and expanded to assure considerably more responsiveness to immediate societal needs, according to 157 of the citizens. To be more precise, they want the institutions of higher learning to produce more medical doctors, nurses, and related technicians. Quality medical care is a principal concern in the nation's third largest city, and as one citizen said, "It is a real hassle to get your family adequate medical service. There are not enough doctors and supporting personnel to go around." He supported an expanded program of medical education by asking, "How many unemployed doctors and nurses do you know about?" He, incidentally, was an unemployed electrical engineer. More than half of the group questioned the wisdom of turning out many more graduates from certain of the more traditional programs in arts and sciences. It was obvious that the majority favored those institutions which produced graduates capable of offering needed services and paying taxes. Professional and technical schools were cited with regularity. Medical and allied health programs continue to enjoy preferential status, but no fewer than two dozen of the participants wondered whether academia might not be on the verge of over-producing even in this field. One hundred eighty-one of the 200 are opposed to the production of Ph.D.s at existing rates. They view the current situation with alarm and believe it to represent a substantial waste of public funds and talented personnel. Only two of the people saw no need for realignment on the campus, and one of them was a professor of English at Northwestern University. The practitioner of educational administration must acknowledge that academic change and political reality are correlated in a number of ways, much to the chagrin of the pure academic.

4. *Are faculty members being compensated fairly?*

External, or off-campus, perceptions of today's college professor are far from complimentary, according to two-thirds of the surveyed people. In their judgment, he is a highly able individual who has been rewarded in a generous manner, especially in the last ten years. They see the professor as being ungrateful and unwilling to recognize the economic duress of the day. They see him as one who has no sense of perspective. One hundred forty of the participants were critical of the professor's current moves toward collective bargaining. Several fear that unionization of college faculty might lead to a sterilization of American higher education. There is general misunderstanding of what constitutes a faculty member's work load. Nearly half of the people thought that the average professor probably was overpaid and underworked. Convincing the general public of faculty economic need will be no easy task in the immediate years ahead, especially with more and more academics being persuaded that their only chance for fiscal equity must come in the form of demands through unionization. A housewife and mother of two University of Illinois students observed that "only the faculty member is held in less esteem than the administrator." One hundred sixty-five of the 200 regarded the professor as being "permissive" with young people. They admitted to respecting his intellect, but questioning his values.

5. *What marks would you give today's college students?*

Just over half of the lay graders gave the majority of collegians a B-plus for deportment. Although high, their grades were representative of a new era of conciliation which has informed educational observers claiming that college students are more accepted now than at any time since the early 1960s. This is not to imply that a majority of the representative sampling favors the long hair of the 1970s over the crew cuts of the 1960s. Reasons for the change in attitude are explicit. Cooling of student tempers in recent years has brought appreciably more public acceptance to the academic community. Both Gallup and Harris have found that the average American citizen has little time or sympathy for disfranchised students who express themselves through unruly demonstration.[5] Politicians, both large and small, conservative and liberal, have refrained from criticizing the student community, waiting to gauge the full impact of the eighteen-year-old vote. One hundred twenty-two of the polled citizens are convinced that the newfound level of acceptability is attributable to the student's immediate access to political change or the ballot box. Suddenly, they believe, the student became a political necessity rather than a political liability. It is interesting to note that over half of the people were unwilling to criticize college students for their long articulated opposition to the Vietnam war. Some of them, in fact, said history might prove that the students were right on the Vietnam issue.

6. *Would you be concerned in sending a son or daughter to today's campus?*

There is universal concern over the reportedly heavy use of drugs at colleges and universities. For example, 140 of those sampled said that they were convinced that an offspring of theirs probably would not indulge, but they fear for general student safety in an atmosphere permeated by drugs. They view the user as a possible threat to the well-being of others. Only 22 people expressed apprehension over the consumption of alcohol on the campus. Several, in fact, volunteered that they would prefer having a son or daughter take a drink rather than experiment with drugs, regardless of the form. Reports of the new morality leave the majority of participants somewhat uncertain and reluctant to say too much. Half of the group did believe that most young people were "moral churchgoers" when they left home for academia. What happens from that juncture, they claim, is beyond their control. They allude to what some perceive as a permissive attitude among faculty and an unwillingness of administrators to take tough stands. It became evident that the majority favored a more disciplined academic setting. That discipline, if it is to be realized, will have to be fostered by the collegiate administrator, they believe. Interestingly, 124 of those surveyed feel that the reported depreciation of traditional values among the young is overstated by the media. They see the average collegian as being too liberal, somewhat irresponsible, but clearly promising. They see much of themselves — ten, twenty, and thirty years removed — in the youth of today, only parts of the image are blurred by the more radical oratory and appearance of the 1970s.

7. *How should state and federal government share the cost of public higher education?*

The sampling illustrates that an average taxpayer feels "put upon" by the heavy fiscal demands of public colleges and universities. He further feels that the time of spiraling budgets for higher education is past. More than two-thirds of the polled citizens assume that the state of Illinois, despite its massive industrial base, cannot afford to increase appreciably its support of the institutions of higher learning. They admit to wanting tax relief at the state level, as do citizens in other states. If there is to be increased revenue for higher education, it should come from non-state tax resources, 155 of the people believe. Their suggestion is for colleges and universities to explore the possibilities of added support from the federal government and private foundations, which they see as having a fundamental stake in the plight of academia and immediate access to adequate resources. There was some feeling that official Washington has not been as generous with higher education as it might have been, but one needs to know that over half of the Chicago group believe the academy already is financed handsomely and faces no real economic crisis. It is a matter of restructuring priorities, they say. All but eleven of the people thought that the control of state colleges and universities should remain lodged with the state despite the magnitude of the on-going financial commitment. The thought of possible federal control of higher education leaves the majority uneasy and overtly defensive. There is growing sentiment that the federal government should assume more of the economic burden for the training of medical doctors and health-related personnel, as well as other professional programs which are inordinately expensive and intricately tied to the general welfare of society.

8. *Should private colleges and universities be preserved?*

Belief in the need for private institutions of higher learning is commonly held and freely expressed, yet 79 percent of the citizens expressed preference for the public campus. They would prefer to send a son or daughter to a publicly financed college or university. Despite the private sector's emphasis on more personalized instruction and greater interaction between student and faculty member, the majority feels that the quality of academic programing is superior at the public institution because of more generous funding. Ten years ago, they sensed no difference in quality. Thus, two-thirds of the participants endorsed the concept of state and federal assistance for private higher education. Aside from the issue of academic quality or equity, they are persuaded that it would be more economical to assist private colleges and universities so that they might accommodate most of the future growth in student numbers. There is little support for expansion of the public, four-year institutions, which many believe are already far too large and far too impersonal.

Among the other salient findings were:

1. Higher education's principal asset is its past record service, but over half of the Chicago sampling warned that academia cannot live on its laurels indefinitely.

2. There is strong sentiment that collegiate programs must be alerted in terms of responsiveness to social and economic needs. Over 100 of the citizens believe that the existing curriculum is somewhat dated and irrelevant to a number of today's problems.

3. The general public does not have an adequate voice in the higher educational enterprise. According to the expressed view of the majority, boards of trustees tend to represent special groups and not general concerns.

4. There is no consensus on how to assure more representative governing boards. Sixty-one citizens favored the elective process,

55 preferred appointment, and the remaining 84 gave no specific recommendations on the matter.

5. Colleges and universities should pare their graduate offerings, especially in areas where employment prospects are marginal. One hundred thirty-two of the people believe academia has been irresponsible in the production of either unemployed or underemployed Ph.D.s.

6. Community or junior colleges should be encouraged to continue to grow, especially in the field of vocational and technical education. Two-thirds of the sampling equate the two-year programs with the realization of essential manpower needs.[6]

NOTES

1. Thirty-one of the nation's governors participated in an educational survey which was conducted by the authors in May of 1972. One hundred forty legislators from twenty-five states also responded to the questionnaire.

2. *Chicago Tribune*, October 9, 1960, p. 1.

3. In determining the relevance of academic issues and the ensuing questions, the authors received the generous assistance of staff officers at the American Council on Education, Washington, D.C. The survey was conducted in October and November of 1972.

4. *Washington Post*, September 21, 1972, p. 3.

5. *New York Times*, February 7, 1972, p. 11.

6. Ten college and university presidents from five states — California, Kansas, New York, Ohio, and Texas — reviewed the survey results and found them to be realistic, representative of their geographical regions, and illustrative of the problems facing their program efforts. They see few easy solutions but believe the next five years could bring new and needed understanding of the academy and its aspirations. One of the presidents called for "an academic reconstruction period" ig American higher education, a time when the academic and the citizen could work together in building a more viable educational structure.

SUPPLEMENTARY REFERENCES

BEREDAY, GEORGE Z. *Education and Economic Development.*
Lincoln: University of Nebraska Publication, 1970.

BUDIG, GENA A., editor and contributor. *Budgeting for Today's
Campus.* Chicago: College and University Business Press,
McGraw-Hill Publications Company, 1972.

CARNEGIE COMMISSION ON HIGHER EDUCATION. *The Capital and
the Campus: State Responsibility for Post Secondary Education.* New York: McGraw-Hill Book Company, 1971.

CHAMBERS, M. M. *Appropriations of State Tax Funds for Operat-
ing Expenses of Higher Education.* Washington, D.C.: National
Association of State Universities and Land-Grant Colleges,
1969.

GLENNY, LYMAN. "Statewide Planning for Post Secondary Education," materials prepared for a National Research Training
Seminar. Washington, D.C., 1971.

86843